The Knights

Robin Griffith-Jones
Master, The Temple Church

✠

The Knights Templar were one of the two most powerful military-religious orders of medieval Europe. Only the Knights Hospitaller rivalled them. The Templars evolved from the call by Pope Urban II for the Christian kings and knights of Europe to recover for Christians the burial place of Christ in the holy city of Jerusalem and to 'liberate the Church of God'. The Templars' rise and their equally dramatic fall in the 1300s have intrigued historians and popular myth-makers alike. With land-holdings and treasuries across Europe and the Middle East, the Templars' wealth was immense. Their military prowess was admired by friend and foe; their religious dedication seemed exemplary; their financial acumen enviable. No wonder their sudden destruction has seemed to later generations mysteriously catastrophic.

The Templars' story began with the First Crusade, when Europe's kings and nobles led armies to answer the pope's call to arms. After they captured Jerusalem in July 1099, the Crusaders founded the Kingdom of Outremer, 'Beyond the Sea'. Christian pilgrims could again visit the Holy Land, though the way was not safe. In or around 1120 a small group of knights took the three monastic vows of poverty, chastity and obedience, and undertook to keep the pilgrim routes safe for Christians. The king of Jerusalem gave them headquarters on the 'Temple Mount', built by Herod the Great over one thousand years before; and so the new Order of knighthood became known as the Knights Templar.

ABOVE: A medieval ideal of piety and power: a kneeling Crusader with his horse behind him. This may be King Henry III of England, who took the cross in 1250. Illustration from the Westminster Psalter, a 13th-century English manuscript.

The Crusades

There were eight major Crusader campaigns and many smaller ventures to the Middle East between 1096 and 1291. In calling on kings and their peoples to join these campaigns, the pope in Rome could appeal to the duties both of knightly service and of Christian love. In feudal Europe, a vassal had to swear loyalty to his liege-lord and defend the lord's honour. To Christian knights, their final liege-lord was no earthly king or baron, but Christ himself, and they were willing to endure privation, danger and death in order to serve their Lord and restore to the Church and its pilgrims the land made holy by his earthly existence.

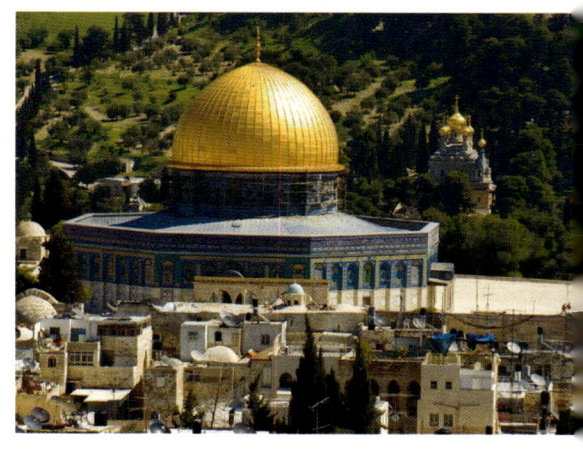

ABOVE: The Dome of the Rock on the Temple Mount in Jerusalem; the Mount of Olives is in the background. The Dome was believed by the Crusaders to be the Temple of the Lord in which Jesus was presented as an infant to God (Luke 2.22–32). The Templars' headquarters, also on the Mount and just 90 metres (300 feet) away, faced the Dome.

RIGHT: Crusaders on board ship, making for the Crusades. Illustration from a 13th-century Spanish manuscript.

FAR RIGHT: Crusaders leaving a fortified city, its defenders watching from the battlements. This 12th-century wall-painting is from the Templars' church at Cressac-sur-Charente, France.

JERUSALEM AND THE FIRST CRUSADE

According to the earliest Islamic traditions, the Noble Sanctuary, site of the Aqsa ('furthest') Mosque, in Jerusalem had been visited by Muhammed. The city, already holy for Jews and Christians, became as a result the third holiest site in Islam. Christian pilgrims visited the city in peace until the 1000s; after this they were safe only under armed escort, and in 1095 Pope Urban II called for a military campaign to secure the Holy Land for Christendom. A 'People's Crusade', ill-disciplined and largely unarmed, set out; its members were massacred or captured before they ever saw the Holy Land. A more organised army arrived in 1096, and entered Jerusalem in 1099. Four states ruled by Christians were set up: the kingdom of Jerusalem, and the principalities of Antioch, Edessa and Tripoli.

Holy war promised redemption. No Christians in the Middle Ages could escape the sense of their own sinfulness; but how to escape punishment for their sins, in the life to come? The Crusades offered one answer: Crusaders were warriors and pilgrims, winning remission for their sins by their commitment to a holy war, and they could turn to scripture for support. Jesus himself had said, 'Everyone that hath left house or brethren or sisters or father or mother or wife or children or lands, for my name's sake, shall receive an hundred-fold and shall possess life everlasting' (Matthew 19.29); and also, 'If any man will come after me, let him deny himself and take up his cross and follow me' (Matthew 16.24). The Crusades offered a new way to follow Jesus – by leaving home and family, heading well over a thousand miles to the East and fighting, in penitence, to win back possession of the Holy Land. Those who undertook to go on Crusade were given a cross, generally of cloth, to 'take up' and wear on their chest until their vow had been fulfilled.

Religious zeal was one engine driving the Crusades. Today we recognise that politics and economics were also motivating forces. The balance of power in the Eastern Mediterranean was shifting. Muslims had controlled Jerusalem and the Holy Land since 638, and Islam had spread westwards through North Africa and into Spain; but by the 1090s the cohesion of Mediterranean Islam had broken down. The Christian Byzantine Empire, centred on Constantinople, no longer dominated the Eastern Mediterranean. There was a power vacuum.

The economic horizons of Western Europe, by contrast, were expanding, as trade brought contacts with Eastern regions neglected since the Roman Empire. There was new interest in the Middle East, and in a trade that would surely prosper if supported by a Christian kingdom at the eastern end of the Mediterranean. Gold and silver were pouring into Europe from the Muslim East. Europe was turning to cash-currency, and needed ever more bullion for its coinage. The wealth of the East was an inviting prospect, feeding ambitions for military campaigns.

It is perhaps too easy, now, to see only the politics and economics of the Crusades, ignoring the fervour and courage of many who fought in them. Among the most deeply committed, most disciplined, and bravest of the Crusaders were 'the poor fellow-soldiers of Christ and of Solomon's Temple' – the Templars.

The Brotherhood

The Crusaders captured Jerusalem from the Muslims in July 1099. Even hardened fighters were struck by the victors' violence. The Temple Mount streamed ankle-deep with the defenders' blood; and three days later many of the surviving Muslims were made to dispose of the bodies and were then themselves killed in cold blood. There was no monopoly on such massacre; recent Turkish conquests in the Near East had involved carnage and mass enslavement, and later Muslim victories (such as Zengi's at Edessa in 1144) would be brutal too. The story of the Templars and their adversaries is inescapably the history, many centuries past, of 'War, and the pity of War'.

Jerusalem was in Christian hands; but pilgrims were still in danger from attack all along their routes in the Holy Land. A French knight, Hugh of Payns, led the band of knights who offered, in or around 1119, to protect pilgrims. The patriarch and the king of Jerusalem accepted their offer. Hugh travelled west to Europe, seeking recognition and recruits. These recruits would be both men of war and men of prayer. It was a strange combination, and the Templars were viewed with some suspicion. But in 1129, Bernard of Clairvaux, one of the age's greatest monks, spoke up for the knights and compiled their formal Rule. He wrote a book, *In Praise of the New Knighthood*, and with Bernard on their side the Templars' future was assured. The Order was duly established under papal authority. The Templars' star had risen.

The Cistercian, Bernard, had in 1115 founded a monastery at Clairvaux, near Hugh's home of Payns, whose members followed a severely ascetic life. Bound by a Rule of Bernard's devising, the Templars, too, were examples of rigour and self-denial, conspicuously devout and prayerful. Their Rule ordained (in monastic style) that they attend seven services a day; the first before sunrise, the last at dusk. Even on campaign they were to say, at the set hours, the Lord's Prayer ('Our Father') several times instead.

There were Templars of different standing within the Order. In general only those recruits of 'knightly' birth could afford the costs of equipping themselves for war on horseback; and the Order came to require Knight-Brothers to be of knightly rank. (The price of horses doubled between 1140 and 1180, and doubled again by 1220.) Those of lower birth became Sergeant-Brothers. The head of the Order was the Grand Master, elected by the Grand Chapter, a body of 13 knights and sergeants. Each house, or Temple, had a commander, owing obedience to the Grand Master. Each knight was entitled to three horses, each sergeant to one. The Sergeant-Brothers, not all of whom were fighting men, greatly outnumbered the Knight-Brothers; both knights and sergeants could rise in the Order by talent and hard work – an important consideration, in a world that was in general rigidly hierarchical.

There were also associates who had committed themselves and their property in various ways to the Order. The Templars' Rule barred women, but women there were: apart from a nunnery in Germany, it is known that several women lived in Templar houses, some apparently sharing the same house as Brothers and some in full

ABOVE: Templars attired in a cloak (left) and a habit (right); they were both soldiers and monks. The belt around the knight's waist represents a vow of chastity.

ABOVE: The initiation of Jacques de Molay into the Order of the Knights Templar, 1295; de Molay became Grand Master of the Temple and was burnt at the stake in 1314. A painting by the French artist F.M. Granet (1775–1849).

LEFT: The Templars' seal (two knights on one horse) and their banner (a black and a white field). Sketch by Matthew Paris (died 1259) in his manuscript *History of the English*; Paris believed that the seal's design had signified the Order's original poverty.

THE TEMPLARS' RULE

Bernard of Clairvaux's Rule of 1129 for the Templars' daily life was written in Latin; further clauses were later added in French (which more of the knights understood), to address the practical questions of life on campaign. The knights' day was modelled on the monastic routine of seven services through the day. There was to be no swearing, no gambling, no drunkenness, no sex, and limited hunting. Showy dress and ornamental horse-trappings were also forbidden. These Rules set the Templars apart from ordinary knights.

obedience to the Rule. Sexual relationships were forbidden; at their entry into the Order the knights bound a cord around their waist, to remind them of their vow of chastity. Templars, most of whom joined for life, committed themselves to poverty; but the Templar Order became very rich and powerful. Houses were modest, but their chapels and liturgy were lavish and beautiful. Their military prowess and wealth were balanced by their calling to a life of discipline and prayer.

Warrior Knights and Pilgrims

The Templars formed the first institutional, professional army within the 'Latin' Christendom of the Roman Catholic West. Each knight was loyal to the Order above all else. The Templars were soon entrusted by Christian rulers in the Holy Land with the defence of key points; King Baldwin III of Jerusalem, for instance, put them in charge of Gaza (1150). A network of castles and their lands ensured the Templars became independent of local rulers.

The Templars and Hospitallers often exercised an influence in battle quite disproportionate to their small numbers. Each probably had, at most, 300–600 knights in the Holy Land at any one time, with 2,000 sergeants and attendants. The knights also hired mercenaries: lightly armed infantry and archers. The Templars provided the vanguard and rearguard on the march, protecting an army advancing through hostile territory; and they defended the camps. In battle, Templar knights fought as heavy cavalry, each knight fully

THE KNIGHTS HOSPITALLER

The Hospitallers, founded in 1070, had by 1099 set up hostels for pilgrims travelling to the Holy Land and were established in Jerusalem, nursing the sick as well as fighting the Muslim forces. After the Latin dominions fell in 1291, the Hospitallers retreated first to Cyprus and then to Rhodes. By 1565 they were based in Malta and survived a siege with epic heroism. In the 19th century, they redefined themselves: they became providers of emergency medical care; and as such, the Order of St John continues to offer first aid and nursing, in peace and war, in Britain and throughout the world.

BELOW: Battle between Muslim cavalry (on the left) and Crusaders (on the right).

armoured on a war-horse; they were trained to charge in tight formation and never to break ranks. Their well-timed charges could win the day. And if not? The knights were famous for the courage with which they fought and fell in battles catastrophically lost.

Templar courage was seldom in doubt. At the Battle of Montgisard (1177), facing the renowned Muslim commander Saladin, the Templars charged straight for Saladin's own battalion. At Damietta (1219), when Muslim warriors breached the city's defences, the Templars rallied the defenders by a sudden charge. In the darkest hours of defeat, Templars fought resolutely: at the Battle of the Horns of Hattin (1187), 230 Templar knights were killed. Templars and Hospitallers urged against joining battle at Mansourah (1250) but were over-ruled; 280 Templar knights including the Grand Master were killed.

Religious devotion inspired such deeds. 'Not to us', called out the Templars as they charged into battle, 'not to us but to you be the glory, O Lord!' The Muslim commanders well knew the value of such devotedly ferocious warriors. Saladin was widely respected by friend and foe for his customary chivalry towards defeated enemies. But there were limits; after his victory at the Horns of Hattin, Saladin offered Templar and Hospitaller prisoners life – if they would convert to Islam. All those who refused were killed.

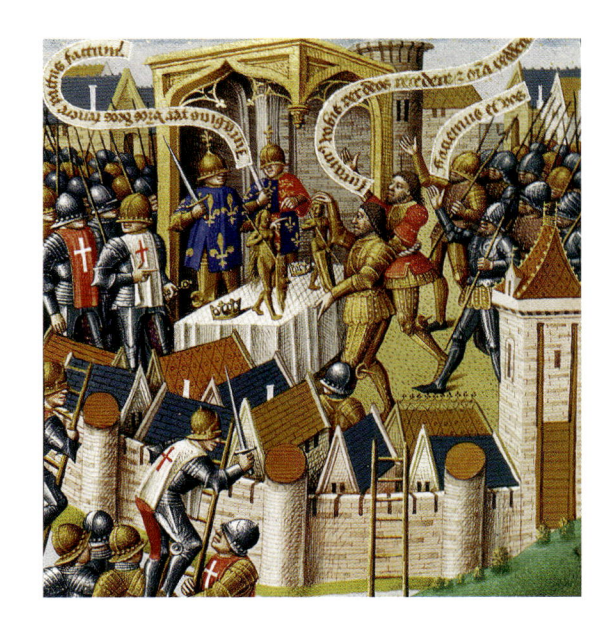

ABOVE: The capture of Acre by the Crusaders, 1191, on the Third Crusade: King Philip II of France and King Richard I 'Lionheart' of England stand together at the altar.

LEFT: Crusaders led by St George driving Muslim cavalry from the field of battle. Illustration beneath a map of Jerusalem and its holy places from a 12th-century manuscript.

THE BATTLE OF THE HORNS OF HATTIN

By the 1170s and 1180s Saladin had won control of all the territory around the Kingdom of Jerusalem. At Hattin in 1187 he tempted the Crusaders' army away from a well-watered encampment onto a forced march through the desert. On 3 July he trapped the Crusaders on a waterless plateau; overnight he lit smoke-filled fires upwind of them, and set archers to rain down arrows on their camp. The next day the Crusaders, exhausted and parched, suffered a crushing defeat. City after city then fell to Saladin; on 2 October he occupied Jerusalem. The news horrified Europe; on 29 October 1187 the pope declared the Third Crusade.

The Templars in the West and the East

The Templars enjoyed privileges from the pope: they were exempt from tithes (taxes), and from the jurisdiction of bishops in sees where they held lands. Such freedoms allowed the Order to grow and diversify, in both the East and the West. From the start the Grand Master and his senior colleagues were focused on the East and were based there; the Grand Master presided in the Great Chapter at which all significant decisions were made. The Order owned and managed extensive houses and estates in Western Europe, which became sources of income and bastions of political power. In a typical year one third of the western income was remitted to the East. In some years far more money was needed; as when the Templars bought the island of Cyprus (1191–92) or the city of Sidon (1260), or when, in later years, they built a fleet.

ABOVE: Convent of Christ Castle in Tomar, a Crusader stronghold in Portugal, built in 1160.

LEFT: Two scenes in a counting-house: counting money (above); and checking the ledgers (below), from a 14th-century Italian manuscript.

THE SECOND CRUSADE

News in 1144 that the Crusaders' state of Edessa had fallen to Turkish Muslims stirred anger and fear in Europe. Bernard of Clairvaux preached a new Crusade, inspiring Louis VII of France and Conrad III of Germany to lead a large army once more to the East. The French and German armies travelled separately across Anatolia; both lost battles on the way. When the surviving troops reached Jerusalem, the Crusaders decided to besiege the city of Damascus. The siege failed disastrously; its different leaders blamed each other, and the Christians' position was worse than it had been before the Crusade.

ABOVE: The vast fortress of Krak des Chevaliers, guarding a valley running across Lebanon to the sea, was given in 1144 to the Knights Hospitaller, who added the outer walls. An enemy who captured these walls could lay siege from them to the inner fortress. In 1271 the Mamluks captured the castle after a siege of just five weeks.

The Order managed its own funds and their movement across political borders so effectively that it was soon managing the funds of others. The Templars' houses were safe, they themselves were honest, and they were experienced in the control of large and complex assets. As early as the 1140s, the king of France could sustain his campaign in the East only through loans arranged by the Templars; ordinary Crusaders came to rely on the Order too. Through most of the 13th century the Paris Temple acted as treasury to the kings of France, and the Order ran accounts – dealing with receipts and payments, deposits and loans – for royalty and nobles.

The Templars' liquidity could be dangerously tempting. In 1250, Louis IX of France, the 'Crusader king', led the Seventh Crusade to disaster in Egypt, where he and his army were captured. The army's treasury was 400km (250 miles) away; without enough gold to pay the king's ransom, royal agents made the Templars, under protest, hand over their depositors' money to make up the shortfall.

The Templars were among the founding fathers of international banking. Their knights were essential to western military operations in the Middle East, but at times they may have seemed more interested in mercantile advantage than in military activity. Louis IX had good reason to be grateful to the Templars; but he was appalled to learn in 1252 that the Templars had secretly agreed a land deal with their favoured ally, the sultan of Damascus. Such pragmatism aroused suspicion, and critics began to question what the Templars were really trying to achieve.

WARS IN EUROPE

The Templars were involved in wars in both Western and Eastern Europe. In the Iberian peninsula, they helped Christian forces in the 'reconquest' of Spain and Portugal from the Muslim Moors. The Order was given land in Portugal as early as 1128; some of the most impressive Templar castles – Almurol, Pombal and Tomar – are in Portugal. Others, such as Peníscola, Ponferrada and Xivert, are in Spain. The Christian forces reclaimed the Iberian peninsula in a long struggle following the years after the Muslims' defeat at Las Navas de Tolosa in 1212. In the 13th century, the Templars were also active in Central Europe, controlling and fortifying border lands threatened by incursions from the East.

'The New Temple' in London

The Templars soon had a base, or house, in London, and by the early 1160s had moved to their second house in the city, 'the New Temple'. The district is still called the Temple today. Its location shows how prestigious the Order had become. The New Temple sits between London's main east-west arteries: the River Thames to the south, Fleet Street to the north. To the east were the merchants, and the wealth, of the City of London; a mile to the west was the City of Westminster, to which the king of England had moved his court and the centre of his government.

London's New Temple was a hub of economic and political activity. The Templars had various enterprises to run: for their own horses, armour and training, a forge and a jousting-ground; for their local business, a tide-mill and a wherry (barge). And in their treasury were the deposits of royalty and barons; in 1307 the new king, Edward II, removed £50,000 of royal treasure from the Temple's treasury – a vast sum.

While the Templars busied themselves in London, their thoughts still turned to the symbolic and spiritual heart of Christendom: Jerusalem. Geographers placed Jerusalem at the centre of the medieval world, and as such it is depicted on maps of the era. The Templars had the city's two greatest buildings forever in mind: one marked Jesus' infancy, the other his death and

LEFT: The Temple Church in London: the Round Church, consecrated in 1185, the Chancel (to the left) in 1240. The column topped by knights was erected in 2000 to mark the new Millennium.

BELOW: Map of Jerusalem and its environs, schematically drawn to the ideas and ideals of western Christendom: perfectly round with a cruciform pattern of streets. A 12th-century manuscript illustration.

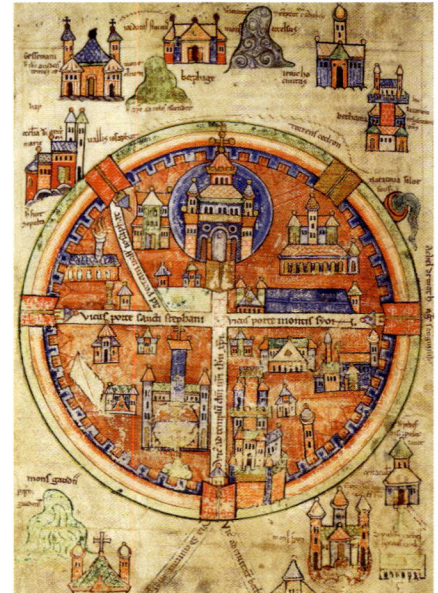

THE BARONS AND THE MAGNA CARTA

In December 1214, King John took refuge in the Temple during his dispute with England's barons; and in June 1215, at Runnymede, he put his seal to Magna Carta, England's first bill of rights. The man who had liaised between John and the barons was William Marshal, Earl of Pembroke; one of Magna Carta's 25 surety-barons (who supervised its enforcement) was William Marshal's eldest son, and one of the witnesses was Aymeric de St Maur, Master of the Temple in England. All three were later buried in the Temple Church; the effigies of the two Marshals survive to this day.

---

resurrection. On the Temple Mount itself, right opposite the Templars' own headquarters, was the octagonal Aqsa Mosque, which the Crusaders believed to be the ancient 'Temple of the Lord' in which the infant Jesus had been presented to God at Candlemas (Luke 2.22–38). And less than a mile away was the destination of every pilgrim: the round Church of the Holy Sepulchre, built in the 4th century by the Roman Emperor Constantine on the site, it was believed, of Christ's death, burial and resurrection. When the Templars built their characteristic round churches they recreated the shape (and so the sanctity) of the Holy Sepulchre itself; and by happy coincidence Heraclius the Patriarch of Jerusalem was in London and could consecrate the New Temple's Round Church at Candlemas 1185.

ABOVE: Effigy in the Temple Church, London, believed to show William Marshal, 1st Earl of Pembroke (1146–1219), the greatest knight of his age and a close friend of Aymeric de St Maur, Master of the Temple in England. William had been on Crusade as a young man and had brought back silks from the Holy Land to be draped over him at his burial. He became a Templar on his deathbed.

BANKERS TO EUROPE

The New Temple in London – the area in which the Temple Church still stands – was a centre of English finance. Successive kings deposited cash here and instructed the Templars on its use. Large sums were often involved: £29,000 in taxes from Nottingham were deposited in 1238; and in 1307 Edward II removed from the Temple £50,000 of silver, together with gold and jewels. Templars were valuable middle-men in transactions throughout Europe and the Mediterranean. A credit note issued in the Middle East, for example, could be presented in Paris for cash – a valuable service for merchants. Just as important for kings on Crusades was the cash that could be raised in the Middle East either from the Templars themselves or from local merchants; the money could be repaid to the tenders or their agents through the Templars' treasuries in Western Europe.

The Templars and the Holy Grail

Did the Templars own and guard the Holy Grail, the cup which Jesus himself had used at the Last Supper with his disciples (Mark 14.22–25)? Or was the Holy Grail not really an object at all but a secret – the bloodline of Jesus, carried on through his descendants to the Middle Ages and beyond? There is, to be honest, more muddle than mystery here; however, to follow the story of the Grail is to follow an important thread in medieval literature.

The Holy Grail is probably an invention of the poet Chrétien de Troyes, who in the 1180s wrote *The Story of the Grail*. Here the Grail is a large shallow dish – the meaning of *graal* – with a single wafer on it, and with magic properties. The wafer recalls the bread which, when blessed at the Christian Mass or Eucharist, becomes 'the Body of Christ'. There are no Templars to guard this Grail.

Twenty years later, Wolfram von Eschenbach in his epic *Parzeval* – heavily indebted to Chrétien – does indeed have the Grail guarded in a Temple by *Templeisen*. But Wolfram's Grail is not a cup either;

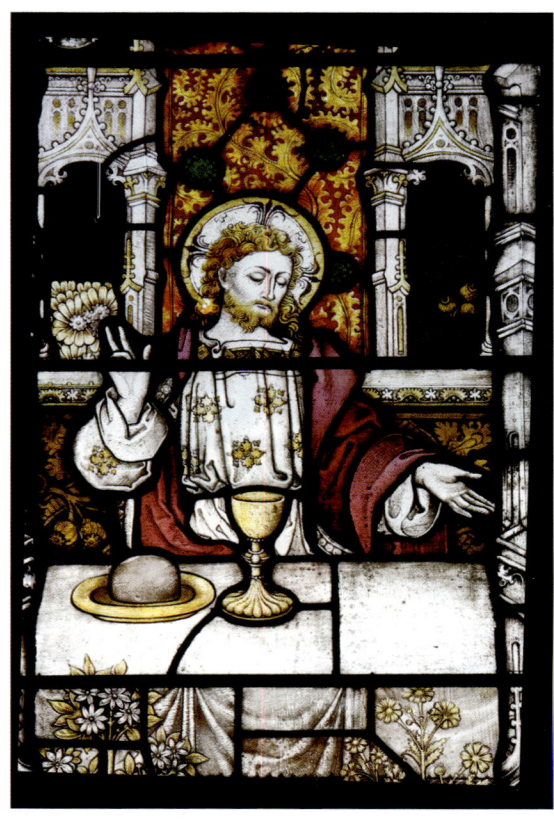

ABOVE: Jesus at the Last Supper, praying over the bread and wine. A 19th-century stained-glass window in the Church of St Michael and All Angels, Uffington, Lincolnshire.

ABOVE: The crucifixion of Jesus. Between Jesus and his mother, Joseph of Arimathea (Mark 15.43) is kneeling to catch Jesus' blood in the Grail. A 15th-century manuscript illustration.

it is a precious stone, decorated with gold. Again, it has magic properties: in its presence food never runs out; anyone who sees it is protected from death for a week; and on Good Friday (the day of Christ's death) a dove flies down from heaven with a wafer and puts it on the stone.

The knights in Wolfram's story are clearly based on the Templars, but the familiar Grail-cup materializes only in the work of a third author, Robert de Boron, who turned Chrétien's Grail into the cup of the Last Supper. He also gave the cup a second role: it had been used to catch the blood of Jesus at the crucifixion. (The wine in the cup or chalice at the Mass or Eucharist, once blessed, becomes 'the Blood of Christ'.) Here is the Holy

THE MEDIEVAL ROMANCES

The deeds of chivalrous knights were the subject of many medieval poems and stories. The *Chanson de Roland* is perhaps the most famous, about a battle (long before the Templars and the Crusades) fought between Franks and Moors in 778. Medieval writers created a mythical framework of fact and fantasy, woven around heroes such as Charlemagne (historical), Arthur (possibly historical but cloaked in mystery), and knights such as Galahad (the exemplary pure knight able to look upon the Holy Grail). Bernard of Clairvaux (who wrote the Templars' Rule) influenced writers of such tales by describing the states by which a person could rise to perfect grace. The Templars, with their ascetic, chaste and military virtues, could seem to embody the chivalric ideal.

Grail as we know it; but Robert's Grail is not guarded by Templars at all.

Wolfram and Robert were both weaving their mythic stories round the magic Grail invented by Chrétien de Troyes; and later authors, no less imaginative, fused Wolfram's Templars with Robert's cup. Once the story was in circulation, a possible pun was noticed. The Holy Cup, *San greal*, had held the true blood, *Sang real*, of Jesus. This play on words was well known in the later Middle Ages, evoking the death of Jesus (and his presence in the Mass or Eucharist), rather than any imagined bloodline. The Grail story, and the Templars' fictional role in it, has captivated generations; but its real beauty lies in the history of literature, not of soldiers or religious relics. The Templars were guardians of Christendom's history, longings and ideals. The Grail was a fitting symbol of all that medieval Europe relied on such knights to defend.

RIGHT: Galahad draws a sword from a stone (left, seen through the door), and then presides at the Round Table in the central 'Perilous Seat'. King Arthur, crowned, sits second from right. In the table's central space the Grail is carried by two small angels. Illustration from a 15th-century manuscript.

LEFT: Sir Galahad: The Quest for the Holy Grail. A scene from the poem 'Sir Galahad', by Alfred Lord Tennyson. Galahad is speaking: 'I leave the plain, I climb the height; / No branchy thicket shelter yields; / But blessed forms in whistling storms / Fly o'er waste fens and windy fields.' A painting by A. Hughes (1832–1915).

Decline and Fall

The Christian hold on the Holy Land was insecure. The Crusaders' lines of supply from Western Europe to the Levant were long, costly and exposed to attack. Dynastic quarrels were endemic and destabilising; popes and western kings were entangled in alliances with and against each other, and each wanted a friend on the throne of Jerusalem. Those few kings who were inspired to lead a Crusade themselves found the Templars at the centre of the enterprise.

By 1189 most of the Crusaders' early gains had been lost; Saladin controlled Jerusalem and much of the Holy Land. In 1192, Richard I 'Lionheart' of England and Philip II of France co-led the Third Crusade. After capturing Acre, Richard was dissuaded from attacking Jerusalem by the Templars and Hospitallers, who advised that the city, even if taken, could not be held. He and Saladin agreed a truce. Richard sold Cyprus to the Templars, to raise cash, and gave them one of his own admirals as Master. Four Templars joined Richard's entourage for the homeward journey, which led to his capture and the payment of a vast ransom, raised in England, for his release.

In 1229 Frederick II, king of Sicily (who had been excommunicated by the pope), re-took Jerusalem during the Sixth Crusade, by treaty. Relations with the Templars (who were answerable directly to the pope) broke down: Frederick tried to take over at least one of their castles, and confiscated Templar property in Sicily. Christians in the Holy Land were falling out with one another, the Muslim armies were too strong to be defeated, and the campaign to hold on to Jerusalem came down to diplomacy and treaties. The Templars knew the East well; new arrivals were less sure-footed. 'Everyone who is a fresh emigrant from western lands,' noted the Muslim writer Usama, 'is ruder in character than those who have become

LEFT: King Richard I 'Lionheart' of England (1157–99, reigned from 1189): on the left, sitting in prison in Germany; and on the right, fatally wounded by a cross-bowman (in the city, top right) at Chalus.

WEST MEETS EAST

The Crusades were important historically for the exchanges between East and West, in commerce and culture. Arab scholarship, which had preserved ancient Greek and Roman texts, influenced European learning, through contacts in Iberia, North Africa, the Byzantine empire, and the Crusader kingdoms. Trade between East and West was stimulated, with ships carrying cargoes of spices, textiles, rugs, glass, exotic foods and other products from the Middle East to ports in the West. Castle architecture was affected too, as western builders studied the stone fortifications of Byzantium and the Arab world.

RIGHT: Two kings of chivalry: King Richard I 'Lionheart' of England jousting with Saladin, ruler of Egypt and Syria; by the 1250s this (legendary) duel was depicted in the apartments of King Henry III. Illustration from the Luttrell Psalter, a 14th-century English manuscript.

acclimatised and have held long association with the Muslims.' For the Templars, as Usama knew, fighting was only half the battle.

By the 1260s, a greater threat emerged in the Mamluks from Egypt. (These had been Slav slaves, and were now a ruling dynasty.) There was little real resistance to their attacks; kings in the West were fighting their own wars, and the pope even diverted Crusaders to fight his own cause in Sicily. In the Holy Land, merchants were leaving; money was running out.

In 1291 the final blow fell. Mamluk forces attacked Acre, the last remaining city of the Latin Kingdom, and 7,000 people fled to the stronghold of the Templars. They held out for 12 days. 'But when the Templars and the others,' wrote a chronicler, 'saw that they had no supplies and no hope of human help, they made their confession, committed their souls to Christ, and rushed out ....' All were slaughtered. The Crusaders' few remaining castles on the mainland soon fell, and the land 'Beyond the Sea' was no more.

The Templars set up a new headquarters in Cyprus. They fortified the island of Ruad, off the Syrian coast, until it too was captured in 1302. They had appointed their first admiral in 1301, a sign that they were planning fresh moves. Though battered, the Templars were determined to fight on. The blow that destroyed them came not from the East, but from the West.

BELOW: The Castle of St Nicolas at the entrance to Mandraki Harbour, Rhodes. After the fall of Acre in 1291, Rhodes was in Christendom's front line of defence. The Hospitallers established themselves on the island, 1306–10, and moved their central convent there in 1309.

Arrest and Trial

The Templars in Western Europe had seemed untouchable. For decades they had managed a large part of the French royal finances. Yet it was a French king, Philip IV, who in 1307 turned on them. Why? The Templars had become a target for envy and suspicion. To some, they seemed greedy and proud. They were self-governing, paid no local taxes, provided no local benefits. After the fall of Acre, what was their purpose? Members of the Great Chapter rarely had time to visit, regulate or reorganise the western houses. A poem written around 1300 questioned why the Templars, 'riding their grey horses or taking their ease in the shade and admiring their own fair locks', were not brought to an end. To bring the Templars to an end is exactly what Philip IV of France set out to achieve.

In September 1307 Philip issued secret orders for the knights' impending arrest. Jacques de Molay, Grand Master of the Temple, was in Paris, campaigning for a new Crusade. On 12 October he had an honoured place in the funeral cortège of the king's sister-in-law. A fly within inches of the spider's web, he suspected nothing.

On Friday 13 October 1307, every Templar in King Philip's realm was arrested, placed in solitary confinement and questioned. King and pope, they were told, knew of their 'errors and corruptions', which were listed: knights at their initiation, it was alleged, denied Christ, spat or urinated on a crucifix, and were then kissed by the knight in charge of the ceremony. There were even accusations of idol-worship. Brothers were promised a pardon if they confessed their guilt and returned to the true Church; otherwise they would be condemned to death for heresy. Most of the Templars were middle-aged or elderly, farm managers not warriors. Confessions came thick and fast. Templar Grand Master Jacques de Molay quickly confessed, and the next day repeated his confession in public.

Pope Clement V, furious that the king had defied papal authority, tried – and failed – to resist the fait accompli. He had apparently been alerted to 'suspect' practices earlier in 1307. In 1308 he sent three cardinals to interview the Templar leaders imprisoned at Chinon. A Vatican document, published in 2003–04, shows that these knights confessed to most or all the charges

ABOVE: The arrest of the Templars, 1307–08. Illustration from a 14th-century French manuscript.

ABOVE: The Templars are charged before Pope Clement V (left) and King Philip IV of France.

RIGHT: The burning of the Templars: 54 brothers were burnt outside Paris on 12 May 1310. One of the men tending the fire is seen shielding his face from the heat. Illustration from a 14th-century French manuscript.

BELOW: The worship of an idol. The Templars were accused of venerating a bearded head of 'Baphomet'; the name is a corruption of the Norman-French word for Muhammed. So the Templars were linked with the (wholly false) European fantasies that Muslims venerated Muhammed's image. A 14th-century manuscript illustration.

and were punishable by excommunication; the pope, however, in view of their free confession and penitence, absolved them from such dire punishment. (The pope did not, as some now claim, declare these Templars innocent; far from it.)

Other kings of Europe slowly and reluctantly followed Philip's lead. Edward II of England wrote to the pope, praising the Templars for the purity of their faith and way of life: 'We cannot believe suspicions of this sort until we are given more evidence of them.'

In France the purge continued. On 12 May 1310, 54 Templars were burnt to death outside Paris, and more followed. The king pressed the pope who, on 22 March 1312, declared that the Order, although not found guilty, was so defamed that it could not carry on; he dissolved the Templars. In 1314 the pope appointed three cardinals to hear de Molay's confession again and finally to pass sentence on him. De Molay, exhausted after years of imprisonment, believed that he would be released; instead, he learned he was to be imprisoned for life. It was too much. He retracted his confession. He would, before speaking out, have known the punishment that would inevitably follow. He was now an 'obdurate heretic'. That evening he and another Templar, Geoffrey de Charney, were burnt at the stake, on an island in the River Seine. Observers reported that de Molay died with a calm courage, confident (he declared) that he would be avenged by God. The Knights Templar were at an end.

17

Heroes or Heretics?

The Templars: innocent or guilty? Almost all historians now think the Templars were innocent of the charges laid against them. Why then did King Philip, grandson of the Crusader Louis IX, attack this Crusading Order? Philip may well have wanted to lead a Crusade himself, having suggested a merger of the Templars and Hospitallers. The separate Orders resisted their merger; and by frustrating the king of France, they earned the enmity of Europe's most powerful man.

There were rumours about the Templars, and in particular about their secret initiations. These led to ribaldry and gossip. That was why in August 1307 the pope had ordered a commission of inquiry. It was disturbing to hear youngsters sing, 'Beware the Templars' kiss!' as Templar knights rode by; homosexual activity was a capital offence at the time. The Templars (innocently) revered saintly relics; a clever prosecutor could make this sound like the (wholly blasphemous) worship of idols. The king of France had become preoccupied with religion after his wife's death in 1305; if he were persuaded that the Templars were guilty, he would indeed act to suppress them, for fear of the punishment that would otherwise be unleashed on his kingdom by God.

Templar wealth made them a target. Philip certainly needed money. He had repeatedly debased the French coinage, while promising to restore the sound currency of Louis IX. He had seized the assets of Italian merchants in France and (in 1306) of the Jews. The Templars, vulnerable to lurid accusations, were a natural next target; and Philip's closest adviser, William de Nogaret, excommunicated in 1303 for plotting against Pope Boniface VIII, was the ideal man to bring them down without any deference to papal rights.

Edward II of England had the English Templars questioned, without torture; there were no confessions. In December 1309, Edward seemed to give permission for some torture but there was no enthusiasm for it. The inquisitors even urged that the prisoners be sent across the Channel to Ponthieu (in English hands, but not subject to English law). By 1311, some substantive confessions were extracted: not, for the most part, confessions of guilt but admissions that the defendant had been so badly defamed by the pope's declarations that he could not purge himself. The Master in England continued to deny all the charges against himself and his Order.

Some charges were clearly designed to taint the Templars, by alleging supposedly Muslim and

LEFT: The Templars appearing for judgement in the Chapter House of Lincoln Cathedral before Bishop John Dalderby of Lincoln. A 19th-century stained-glass window.

RIGHT, ABOVE: The West Front of Lincoln Cathedral, viewed from Lincoln Castle.

RIGHT, BELOW: The Chapter House of York Minster, where the Templars were brought for trial following their arrest and detention in York Castle in March 1310.

FAR RIGHT: The White Tower at the Tower of London; the Templars were transferred here from several cities after their trials had no result.

magical practices. The Order's long exposure to the East may have worked against them. Were they thought too friendly and accommodating to Muslim enemies, rather than hardened by battles against them? Some historians argue that Templar discipline in the West had become slack. Initiation rituals, it may be, had become corrupted in some Templar houses; practices devised to test a Templar's readiness to face torture and humiliation had themselves, perhaps, become

THE TRIALS IN ENGLAND

Edward II arrested the Templars in England in January 1308 after the pope, in November 1307, ordered their arrest throughout Europe. The Templars were taken to the royal castles in Newcastle, York, Lincoln, Cambridge, Oxford, Warwick and Canterbury. Few measures were taken until two papal inquisitors arrived in England in September 1309. The Templars were then assembled at the Tower of London, Lincoln Castle and York Castle to be examined. The inquisitors made little progress. In the absence of substantial confessions, the Templars at York and Lincoln were moved to the Tower of London in 1311. Three renegades from the Order then confessed and were reconciled to the Church. Within days, 57 other Templars sought absolution too. The Master of the Temple in England refused to abjure crimes he had never committed; he died soon afterwards in the Tower of London.

strange and blasphemous. Such corruption in a few houses would have been enough to discredit the Order. Their knights would have travelled, over the years, to other houses across Europe. When questioned, their honest answers would have confirmed the inquisitors' suspicions of widespread malpractice and heresy. Perhaps, just perhaps, behind all the smoke there was a scattering of isolated fires.

The Mysterious Legacy

How many Templars escaped from France? It is known that at least a dozen got away, just before or just after the arrests. It was alleged at trial that one leading knight had fled with 50 horses and set sail with 18 ships, and that another knight had made off with a vast treasure. Where these escapees went we do not know. There is no evidence that any made it, as has been suggested, to America.

There is a modern myth that the refugees sailed around Ireland (a dangerous route in October!) to Scotland, and that Templar knights appeared suddenly at the Battle of Bannockburn in 1314, charged the English and helped win the battle for Robert the Bruce. This is just fantasy. Robert depended on the friendship of the king of France and wanted to be reconciled to the pope; he had no reason to give sanctuary to refugees condemned by both. At Bannockburn, when the battle was already turning in favour of the Scots, a mass of 'yeomen and swains' – retainers, safe until then in the woods behind the Scottish lines – rushed down the hill on foot towards the fighting (and the booty). These men were not Templars.

Even in France, most Templars who confessed to misdemeanours were left to live out their days in peace. Elsewhere, there were almost no executions. A French or English Brother in his twenties in 1307 might still have been managing a monastic farm in the 1330s. In Spain, he could have joined one of the two new knightly orders, under royal and not papal control: the Orders of Christ and of Montesa.

Did anything more survive of the Templars? Did the Templars in Paris control a fabulous treasure, far exceeding the Order's own endowments and income? Was there a portentous secret which Templars had discovered in Jerusalem? Such speculations have multiplied without end since the Templars were 'rediscovered' in the 18th century. The Templars, suppressed by tyrannical kings and popes, had surely been free-thinking proto-Masons. Or, as the most famous of all Crusading forces, they had surely formed the most loyal of the popes' legions. Either way, they were a boon to any propagandist. They have remained the object of wild, unfounded speculation ever since.

Far more exciting and moving than such myths about the Templars is the Templars' own history. They were brave and committed people shaped by their own time and inspired by its ideals. We no longer see the Crusades as they were seen eight hundred years ago. But we can still sense

LEFT: Tomb-slabs in Kilmartin graveyard, western Scotland; the slabs (left and right) incised with knights' figures are medieval. There are many such incised slabs along the western coast of Scotland. Speculation has linked them to the Templars, without very much evidence.